Raphaël Martin
Guillaume Plantevin

WAYLAND
www.waylandbooks.co.uk

LION
KING (OR QUEEN) OF THE JUNGLE?

BIRTH

Lions are born in litters of up to four cubs. Each cub weighs almost two kilos. For the first few weeks, the lioness keeps her cubs in a sheltered den where she nurses them. After about a month, they come out of the den and spend their time playing with other cubs, and feeding from their own mother and from other lionesses in the pride.

ANNOYING HABIT?

Using their tails to swat flies all the time, even in their sleep. Maybe it's to convince people they're awake. After all, the king of the jungle wouldn't want anyone to think he's lazy!

FAVOURITE TRICK?

Chasing young elephants and rhinos right under their parents' noses. Lionesses are bold hunters, one or two will distract the mother animal's attention so the others can catch her baby.

FAVOURITE MEAL?

Seven kilograms of meat a day. Any meat will do, from fresh antelope to old gnu carcasses. If the king is hungry he'll eat anything to survive, including his own children. When a new male takes charge of the pride, he doesn't think twice about killing the younger members and replacing them with his own offspring, either.

LIFESPAN
15 YEARS

2.4 TO 3.3 METRES
FROM NOSE TO TAIL

WEIGHS BETWEEN
120 AND 270 KG

TOP SPEED
60 KPH

SUPERPOWER?

The lioness! The lion may be known as king of the jungle, but a crocodile's jaws are more powerful than a lion's, an elephant is stronger and cheetahs are faster. The lioness, however, is truly fearsome. Lionesses inspire terror across the savannah with their clever hunting strategies, sharp teeth and lethal claws.

MOST SPECTACULAR FEAT?

Ruling supreme in their territory, lording it over areas as vast as 200 sq km and scaring off intruders with their menacing roar.

WEAK SPOT?

Being born blind and helpless. But before long, lion cubs are ready to start hunting, and within six months they're chasing after gnus and gazelles!

WORST FEATURE?

Laziness. While the lionesses are out hunting, the king of the jungle sleeps for about 20 hours a day.

KODIAK BEAR

THE WORLD'S LARGEST CARNIVORE

500 KG

500 GRAMS AT BIRTH

 **LIFESPAN 25 YEARS**

3 METRES STANDING UPRIGHT

 TOP SPEED **50 KPH**

BIRTH

Bears give birth in January or February, to up to three cubs at a time. Each cub weighs only around 500 g, about 1,000 times less than an adult bear. The mother nurses her cubs for a year and a half, by which time they have grown considerably. The cleverest cubs start to hunt by the age of three.

FAVOURITE MEAL?

Salmon! It's a big part of a bear's diet. Kodiak bears owe their enormous size to the amount of protein and fat they eat, they even enjoy dining on elk. The world's largest carnivores like their vegetables too. The islands of the Kodiak archipelago, in Alaska, USA, where the bear lives are rich in lush vegetation.

FAVOURITE TRICK?

Catching salmon in the air. Bears stand guard in the river when the salmon are swimming upstream. As the salmon leap clear of rapids and waterfalls, the bear uses its claws or its mouth to grab the fish.

MOST AMAZING FEAT?

Surviving extreme cold on an empty stomach. When the first snows fall the Kodiak bear seeks refuge in its den, where it hibernates for the winter months. Its body slows right down and the bear lives off its reserves of fat. Even when the temperature drops to -40°C, as it sometimes does in Alaska, the bear doesn't stir, not even to go to the toilet!

WEAK SPOT?

Hunters. With its reputation as a mega-carnivore, the Kodiak bear ought to be safe from predators. But because of its huge size, the bear is sought after by hunters ready to pay up to $20,000 for the chance to bag a prize trophy. About 180 Kodiak bears are killed by hunters each year.

SUPERPOWER?

Sense of smell. Kodiak bears can sniff out a smell from several kilometres away. Their excellent sense of smell makes up for their poor eyesight. Bears are very short-sighted.

SALTWATER CROCODILE
HEAVIEST LIVING REPTILE

WEIGHS UP TO
1.2 TONNES

LIFESPAN **40 YEARS**

UP TO
7 METRES
IN LENGTH

TOP SPEED
25 KPH

ANNOYING HABIT?

Being too fond of people. During the Second World War, hundreds of Japanese soldiers are thought to have been eaten by crocodiles in the swamps of Ramree Island in Myanmar, southeast Asia. Saltwater crocodiles have also been known to devour fishermen in Australia, farmers in the Philippines, and even the odd tourist.

GREATEST FEAR?

Ending up in the cooking pot. Crocodile meat tastes a bit like chicken and makes a delicious meal, especially when it's cooked in a tropical fruit sauce. In Sydney, Australia, you can even order a crocodile pizza, and in the Philippines you can try ice cream made from crocodile eggs!

FAVOURITE MEAL?

Kangaroo, buffalo and occasionally, pet dogs. Crocodiles have a huge appetite and eat anything that has flesh and bone. They eat rocks too, to help their stomachs break food down. Birds have a similar digestive system, with a special area of the stomach called the gizzard, where bits of stone and gravel help to grind up food.

WORST FEATURE?

Laziness. Crocodiles spend a lot of time sleeping. But this is actually a good thing. The crocodile saves its energy like this and can go for months without food.

WEAK SPOT?

There are some dangers a crocodile's scales can't protect it from. In fact, because of its scales, the crocodile has become an endangered species. Skin from a crocodile's belly is one of the most expensive skins in the world. Even though it is heavily regulated, some top designers still use crocodile skin to make shoes and handbags. They're not cheap, though. You'd have to spend at least £7,000 to buy a crocodile handbag.

SUPERPOWER?
Making itself invisible. A crocodile can stay absolutely still just under the surface of the water for hours, with only its eyes and nostrils showing, ready to take its victims completely by surprise.

GREAT WHITE SHARK
NOT AS SCARY AS YOU THINK ...

2 TONNES

LIFESPAN 30 YEARS

UP TO
6 METRES
IN LENGTH

TOP SPEED
40 KPH

WORST ENEMY?

Man. Shark-fin is a popular dish in many parts of the world. Every year, about a hundred million sharks are caught and killed for their fins, but sharks only kill between five and fifteen humans a year, usually by mistake. It's still not a good idea to get too close to a shark, though. And don't try feeding them!

WEAK SPOT?

Its snout. Divers discovered to their amazement that they could make a shark stay still by stroking its snout. Rubbing the shark's nose seems to put it into a kind of trance.

WORST HABIT?

Shutting down the Internet. Sharks like to chew on underwater cables. Telecom companies have to use specially reinforced cables to protect them against these cyberpirates of the deep.

FAVOURITE MEAL?

Seals and other pinnipeds (animals with flippers instead of legs). Sharks have between four and six rows of razor-sharp teeth to help them devour their prey.

MOST SPECTACULAR FEAT?

Long-distance swimming. In 2005, a female shark was tagged and tracked over more than 10,000 km in nine months: that's the same distance as a round trip from South Africa to Australia.

GREATEST WEAKNESS?

Eyesight. Sharks are long-sighted, which means they don't see very well close-up. And whatever its reputation, 'Jaws' is not particularly keen on human flesh. If a shark does take a bite of a surfer's leg, it's usually because it has mistaken the surfboard for its favourite prey, the seal.

SUPERPOWER?

Sharks have special sensing organs called *ampullae of Lorenzini*. Linked to the area around the nose by tiny canals, these organs analyse electrical impulses and give the shark a sixth sense that helps it to locate prey from a distance. The shark senses the movement of an animal's heartbeat and muscle contractions. Shark radar works well in the dark, and it can even help the shark to find fish hidden in the sand.

ORCA
THE KILLER WHALE

WEIGHT 7 TONNES

UP TO
8 METRES
IN LENGTH

LIFESPAN
60 YEARS

TOP SPEED **45 KPH**

FAVOURITE TRICK?

Making waves. How do you get a seal off an ice floe? Work in a group and make huge ripples in the water to submerge the ice and dunk the seal. Then, quick as a flash, grab your prey. Orcas like to play with their food before devouring it.

BIRTH

With newborn orcas weighing in at around 200 kg, it makes sense that females only give birth to one baby at a time. And that baby needs to be fed on its mother's milk for about two years.

WORST NIGHTMARE?

Being taken into captivity. For years, orcas have been used for whale shows in theme parks all over the world. But for a predator used to the freedom of the oceans, it must be distressing to be kept in a swimming pool. Scientists believe these highly intelligent animals suffer in captivity: the orcas are incredibly bored and can even be heard crying. It's much better for the orcas if people enjoy watching them out at sea, in their natural habitat.

FAVOURITE MEAL?

Anything! With no natural predators, orcas are at the very top of the food chain. They can eat what they want, and feast on seals, birds, squid, penguins and sometimes even baby whales. Orcas need 60 to 80 kg of meat a day, so it's just as well they're not fussy eaters. In the wild, orcas spend about 90 per cent of their time hunting for food

MOST SPECTACULAR FEAT?

Attacking great white sharks. A daring feat that very few creatures are bold enough to attempt. No wonder the orca is known as the supreme predator of the oceans. No other animal ever dares to attack the orca.

SUPERPOWER?

Mounting organised attacks in groups. Orcas have hunting techniques that are handed down from one generation to the next. One amazing example is storming the beach to catch seals. Orcas hide under water and slide up on to the sand where they beach themselves before grabbing the seals, taking them completely by surprise.

LEATHERBACK TURTLE
A VERY THICK SKIN

WEIGHS UP TO
900 KG

LIFESPAN
30
YEARS

1,000 EGGS PER YEAR

UP TO
1.6 METRES
IN LENGTH

TOP SPEED
35 KPH

BIRTH

When it's time to have her babies, the female leatherback hauls herself on to the beach and buries her eggs in the sand. She can lay as many as 1,000 eggs in a year. The babies hatch and swarm into the sea, but a large number of them rush straight into the claws of waiting crabs, while others get snapped up into seagulls' beaks.

FAVOURITE TRICK?

Hiding their eggs. Crabs, dogs and humans all love to eat turtle eggs. The mother turtle comes ashore to lay her eggs and buries them in the sand well beyond the reach of the waves. She covers her tracks in the sand with her oar-shaped flippers and to really confuse predators, she sometimes takes a few detours on the way back to the sea.

SILLIEST MISTAKE?

Mistaking plastic bags for jellyfish. When a leatherback swallows a plastic bag it is unable to spit it out and chokes to death. Plastic bags are largely to blame for leatherbacks becoming a critically endangered species. Pollution, the destruction of their habitat and climate change have all contributed to the decline in the number of leatherbacks, too.

FAVOURITE MEAL?

Jellyfish. Leatherbacks can munch their own weight in jellyfish in one day. Their digestive system is lined with spikes that help them to digest this tough dinner. They swim thousands of kilometres in search of prey and can find their way around the depths of the ocean almost 1,500 metres below the surface.

SUPERPOWER?

A solid shield. Leatherbacks don't have shells, but they do have a *carapace*, a thick leathery hide shaped like a lute – a musical instrument similar to a guitar. Made of skin and bone, the carapace is almost impossible to cut through. Only orcas and sharks dare attack the leatherback, usually going for the turtle's weakest point, its head. Unlike the tortoise, the leatherback can't retract its head.

HIPPOPOTAMUS
FREE-DIVING CHAMPION

LIFESPAN **50 YEARS**

WEIGHS UP TO
4.5 TONNES

UP TO
5 METRES
IN LENGTH

TOP SPEED
40 KPH

BIRTH

These days, some human mums have water births, but for hippos giving birth under water is as old as the hills. Hippo calves feed under water too, diving down to suckle from their mother and coming up for air every so often. Baby hippos weigh about 45 kg at birth and believe it or not, hippos and whales are distant cousins: they share a common African ancestor.

ANNOYING HABIT?

Always yawning. But don't be fooled into thinking a yawning hippo is feeling sleepy. When a hippo puts its head back and yawns, it's a sign of aggression. And if any challengers are spoiling for a fight, one look at the hippo's teeth is usually enough. A hippo's canines can be as long as 60 cm. And they're not meant for munching on food. Those fangs are a fearsome weapon.

FAVOURITE TRICK?

Water sports! Hippos in Gabon, Central Africa, like to go body surfing. They travel for long distances riding the ocean waves. It's a clever way of heading for new places to graze without having to work too hard to get there.

MOST IMPRESSIVE FEAT?

Getting incredibly fat on a diet of vegetables! How do they do it? By lazing around all day in the water to save energy, and choosing the best grasses and plants for keeping themselves nicely fattened up!

WORST FEATURE?

Hippos are highly strung creatures. It's not a good idea to dip even your little toe into the hippo's waters. Male hippos have violent fights to defend their section of the riverbank and protect their females. They don't think twice about crushing a fallen enemy and often fight to the death. If you want to come back alive from your safari, it's best not to get too close to a hippo. More people are killed in Africa by these herbivorous mammals than by lions. Hippos are definitely not gentle giants!

SUPERPOWER?

Hippos can hold their breath under water for about 15 minutes. When they dive, their nostrils close automatically to block out the water.

AFRICAN ELEPHANT

HEAVYWEIGHT CHAMPION OF THE WORLD

WEIGHS UP TO
4.5 TONNES

LIFESPAN **70 YEARS**

4 METRES
IN HEIGHT

TOP SPEED
40 KPH

ANNOYING HABIT?

Spraying itself with dust, and giving everyone nearby a dust bath at the same time. But it's not done just to annoy. Elephants are bothered by parasites that get under their skin, and dust baths are a good way of warding them off.

BIGGEST WEAKNESS?

Being drunk and disorderly. Elephants like fruit and are particularly fond of fermented marula fruit from the elephant tree, which grows in Africa. But with more blood in its body than any other living mammal (several hundred litres), you'd think an elephant would need more than a few pints of fermented marula to get drunk. So why do elephants sometimes stagger around? It's probably from eating too much tree bark. Small, toxic insects in the bark are most likely responsible for the elephant's drunken behaviour.

MOST IMPRESSIVE FEAT?

Weightlifting! An elephant's trunk is extremely strong. Elephants can use their trunk to lift weights of up to 300 kg, the equivalent of about one twentieth of their body weight. Impressive, but nothing compared to the tiny ant, which is capable of carrying as much as twenty times its own body weight.

BEST FEATURE?

An elephant never forgets, or so the saying goes. It's certainly true that elephants are highly intelligent. They use tools, help each other out, and even recognise their own reflection in a mirror. Female elephants, in particular, have incredible memories, and can remember the faces of both humans and other elephants. An elephant's brain is huge, but relative to the size of its body, it's smaller than a mouse's.

SUPERPOWER?

Drinking, fighting, tickling, the elephant's trunk does just about anything you can think of. And if you tried to guess the number of muscles in the trunk, you'd almost certainly be wrong. There are tens of thousands of them.

RHINOCEROS
IRON-CLAD BEAST

WEIGHS UP TO
3.6 TONNES

UP TO **4 METRES** IN LENGTH

TOP SPEED **40 KPH**

LIFESPAN **45 YEARS**

BIRTH

A baby rhino weighs about 40 kg. Mothers feed the babies for one or two years, but that doesn't stop young rhinos from grazing a bit on the side as they follow their mother around. Rhinos love their food!

FAVOURITE TRICK?

Doing a U-turn at top speed. Quite a feat for an animal that weighs as much as a small van!

WORST ENEMY?

Money. Used as a miracle cure in many parts of the world, rhino horn is highly valued. One kilogram of rhino horn can sell for as much as £41,000. Some species of rhino are seriously endangered, and rhino poaching has played a major part in their decline.

MOST IMPRESSIVE FEAT?

Having a portrait painted by an artist who had never seen a rhino. In 1515, the German painter Albrecht Dürer heard people talking about an amazing animal given to the King of Portugal by an Indian sultan. Based only on descriptions given to him by people who'd seen it, Dürer created a woodcut print. The rhino was later given to the pope and died in a shipwreck on the way to its new home. But the picture is still famous today.

FAVOURITE MEAL?

Mixed salad. Rhinos eat all kinds of plants, even the ones covered in spines. The rhino has a hook-like upper lip that allows it to munch on the spikiest of plants without hurting itself.

BEST FRIEND?

Oxpeckers, tiny birds that feed on ticks and other parasites that live on the rhino's skin.

SUPERPOWER?

Perfuming its territory. The rhino likes to trample in its own dung and walk around on its smelly hooves to mark out its territory. It can also use its tail to jet-propel its poo. Message received: keep out!

KOMODO DRAGON
LETHAL LIZARD

WEIGHS UP TO
150 KG

UP TO
3 METRES
IN LENGTH

LIFESPAN
30 YEARS

TOP SPEED
20 KPH

BIRTH

Female Komodo dragons lay between 15 and 30 eggs at a time, which take 8–9 months to hatch. Baby dragons emerge from their eggs at the end of the rainy season. They slice through the shell using their egg tooth, a small sharp horn that falls off after they have cut their way out of the egg.

SILLIEST MISTAKE?

Eating the wrong thing. When they're not eating their own babies, Komodos occasionally decide to dine on nearby villagers. Gulp! One 83-year-old grandmother was having none of it. When a Komodo grabbed hold of her arm she gave the beast a good kick. The dragon was so surprised it let go. Fortunately Komodos only live on one or two remote islands in Indonesia and attacks like this don't happen too often.

FAVOURITE TRICK?

Camouflage. Young Komodos cover themselves in dung as protection from hungry adults, who like to eat the young dragons for dinner. Better safe than sorry!

FAVOURITE MEAL?

Everything! Komodos eat almost anything, from birds to wild boar, and their favourite dish is water buffalo. With their long, forked tongue they sense the smells all around them and locate their prey. Komodo dragons' patience, and ability to blend into their surroundings, makes them successful hunters.

MOST IMPRESSIVE FEAT?

Attracting tourists from all over the world. Thousands of people flock to Indonesia each year to see the dragons.

SUPERPOWER?

Patience. The world's largest lizards aren't in a hurry. They can go for a whole month without eating. Water buffalo are usually too big for Komodos to kill with their jaws, so when a dragon decides to prey on a buffalo, it simply bites its victim and settles down to wait. The wound becomes infected and when the buffalo dies several days later, the Komodo's patience is rewarded.

DEATHSTALKER SCORPION
AS DEADLY AS IT SOUNDS?

WEIGHS UP TO
15 G

10 CM
IN LENGTH

**LIFESPAN
5 YEARS**

TOP SPEED
2 KPH

BIRTH

Deathstalker scorpions give birth to about 50 babies at a time. The mother helps her babies climb up onto her back where they stay clinging on for a few weeks. Their outer shell, or exoskeleton, doesn't grow with them and they have to shed it several times as they grow. They leave their mother after shedding it for the first time, and have to find their own food and place to live.

ANNOYING HABIT?

Hiding in people's clothes! If you go camping in this scorpion's territory, make sure you shake out your sleeping bag before you get into it. A scorpion's sting is very painful, and although it won't necessarily kill a healthy adult human, it can be fatal for the elderly or for people who are ill. Oh, and don't forget to check your shoes before you put them on, too!

FAVOURITE TRICK?

Motion sensors. Deathstalkers have special sensors for detecting vibrations in the ground. They lie in wait, using their sensors to locate approaching prey. When the victim comes within reach, the deathstalker ambushes it, grabbing the prey with its pincers and delivering a dose of venom.

FAVOURITE MEAL?

Spiders, millipedes and crickets are top of the menu.

And female deathstalkers sometimes eat male scorpions, too!

BEST FEATURE?

Being a medical miracle. Deathstalkers can kill, but they have healing properties too. Scientists have succeeded in using their venom to help to identify brain cancer cells: it may be soon possible to target cancers without destroying healthy cells.

SUPERPOWER?

A nasty stinger. When the deathstalker captures its prey, the stinger releases a cocktail of poisonous substances. Deathstalkers in captivity are raised in specially secured glass cages and handlers have to use long pincers measuring at least 20 cm.

BLUE WHALE
LARGEST LIVING ANIMAL

LIFESPAN
80 YEARS

30 METRES IN LENGTH

WEIGHS UP TO
190 TONNES

AVERAGE SPEED
20 KPH

BIRTH

A blue whale pregnancy lasts about a year. When the calf is born, it weighs around two tonnes and is 7 metres long. It needs about 500 litres of milk a day.

ANNOYING HABIT?

Loud honking. Whales have a breathing hole called a blowhole. When the whale comes to the surface it uses the blowhole to blow air out of its lungs.

SILLIEST MISTAKE?

Getting beached near a town. When a whale dies and gets washed up on a beach, it's not easy to move. As the whale decomposes, the gases released can make its carcass (the body of the whale) blow up like a balloon and even sometimes explode.

WORST ENEMY?

Harpoon cannons. A weapon so deadly it almost wiped out the entire species. The blue whale was saved just in time in the 1960s by a ban on hunting it.

BEST FRIENDS?

Save the Whale campaigns. To protect whales from hunters, anti-whaling groups have even gone into battle at sea against illegal whaling ships.

FAVOURITE MEAL?

Blue whales can't get enough of krill, a kind of miniature shrimp. An adult whale needs about 30 to 40 million of them a day. That's a meal weighing several tonnes!

WEAK SPOT?

Being too easy to catch. Before becoming a protected species, blue whales were chased by whale hunters almost to the point of extinction.

SUPERPOWER?

Whale song. Whales can emit sounds as loud as a rocket taking off. Their song travels thousands of kilometres around the globe and is a good way of communicating under water. But with so many noisy ships on the oceans, it is getting more and more difficult for whales to hear each other.

CHEETAH
LAND SPEED RECORD HOLDER

LIFESPAN 10 YEARS

TOP SPEED
112 KPH

1.10 TO 1.50 M
FROM NOSE TO TAIL

AVERAGE WEIGHT
50 KG

MOST IMPRESSIVE FEAT?

Speed. A cheetah in captivity reached a speed of 112 kph. But like all great sprinters, cheetahs can't maintain their top speed for too long: they accelerate very quickly and run in short bursts.

BIRTH

Cheetah cubs are usually born with three or four brothers and sisters. These cuddly little babies weigh only 250 g and are so defenceless that their mother has to move them around constantly to protect them from predators. The babies have a coat of silvery fur that helps to camouflage them in the long grass.

FAVOURITE MEAL?

Antelope. The cheetah's favourite item on the menu is also a very fast runner and the cheetah has to be able to outrun it. And being a great athlete, the cheetah needs an average of 2–3 kg of meat a day.

FAVOURITE TRICK?

Catching their prey by tripping them up as they run. Cheetahs use a special, very sharp claw called a due claw to hook the animal. Once the prey is down, the cheetah strangles it.

WEAK SPOT?

Running out of breath very quickly. A cheetah often loses its prey. When the cheetah stops to catch its breath, lions, hyenas and vultures grab the prey and help themselves. And if it's not quick to make itself scarce, the cheetah itself sometimes gets caught. Which explains why cheetahs usually hunt in the middle of the day, while other big cats are having an afternoon nap.

SILLIEST MISTAKE?

Being impaled on a warthog's tusks. Cheetahs prey on warthogs, but with its pointed tusks a warthog can stop a hungry cheetah running at 70 kph in its tracks.

SUPERPOWER?

An athletic body. The cheetah's powerful heart pumps blood to its finely tuned muscles. Its claws, which don't retract, grip the ground and stop it from skidding as it accelerates. Tight turns? The cheetah can swerve from side to side using its tail as a stabiliser to keep it on track. Its skeleton is light and supple and its paws can stretch so far that the cheetah can cover up to 8 metres in one bound.

ONAGER
BORN TO RUN

TOP SPEED
70 KPH

2 METRES
FROM NOSE TO TAIL

AVERAGE WEIGHT
250 KG

LIFESPAN
20 YEARS

WORST ENEMY?

Trains. The railway line linking Beijing, in China, to the Mongolian capital of Ulaanbaatar stops the onager from travelling to its favourite grazing spots. This wild Asian donkey only needs a bit of wild grass and some fresh water, but it doesn't have an easy life. It has to travel long distances in search of food and water, contend with animals stealing its grazing land and water sources, and poachers hunting it for its hide.

WEAK SPOT?

Poachers. Onagers are hunted both for their meat and for their organs, which are used in traditional medicines in Asia. Poaching is a real threat to the onager, and there are now only around 400 left in the wild. They have also been badly affected by diseases passed on to them by farm animals.

FIFTEEN MINUTES OF FAME

The skin of these wild donkeys used to be an excellent source of fine paper, called parchment. It became famous when a French writer called Honoré de Balzac wrote a novel about a man who found a magic piece of onager skin, a parchment that granted all the owner's wishes. But every time a wish was granted, the parchment shrank and the owner's life was shortened, until the parchment disappeared to nothing and the man died.

WORST FEATURE?

Biting. Onagers can be aggressive and suspicious, and they like to chomp. When the herd is grazing, one of them stands guard and warns the others at the first sign of danger. They are also almost impossible to tame. But when you think of all they have to put up with, you can understand them being so unfriendly.

SUPERPOWER?

High-speed galloping. The onager is not very well known, but by rights, it should be a star. It can run fast enough on its short legs to beat the fastest racehorses in the world – onagers can move at up to 70 kph.

KANGAROO
HEAVYWEIGHT CHAMPION

LIFESPAN
7
YEARS

TOP SPEED
60 KPH

FULL HEIGHT
1.70 M

WEIGHS UP TO
90 KG

her pouch by following a trail of saliva left there by her a few hours earlier.

BEST FEATURE?

Its tail, which a kangaroo uses for steering and balance, almost like a fifth leg. It also allows the kangaroo to hop along at great speed. The only problem is that the tail also gets in the way and stops the kangaroo from moving backwards.

ANNOYING HABIT?

Temper tantrums. The normally peaceful male kangaroo gets very angry when there's a fight over a female. And then it's gloves off, fighting with fists and feet. Anything goes: kicking, punching, shoving – it's a real free-for-all.

SILLIEST MISTAKE?

Having boxing matches in residential areas. In Australia, a homeowner filmed a spectacular fight between two male kangaroos right in front of his house.

FAVOURITE TRICK?

Luring its enemies out of their depth. Kangaroos often fall foul of dingoes, the wild dogs of the Australian bush. The kangaroo's defence is to go and stand in deep water and wait until the dingo is out of its depth, putting the champion boxer at a distinct advantage.

WORST ENEMY?

The Tasmanian tiger, a large, striped predator, was the kangaroo's worst enemy at the beginning of the twentieth century, but that's now extinct. Unluckily for the kangaroo, both dingoes and people still like to eat kangaroo meat.

MOST SPECTACULAR FEAT?

First climb. A baby kangaroo is only 1 or 2 centimetres at birth and weighs not much more than a bee. The tiny baby, called a joey, manages to climb up its mother's fur coat and make its way into

KANGAROO YOU SAID?

Fact or fiction? When English sailors first set eyes on this strange, unfamiliar beast, they asked the locals what it was. Allegedly, the reply was something that sounded like 'kangaroo'. So the urban myth goes that 'kangaroo' is Aboriginal for 'I don't understand'.

SUPERPOWER?

Strong hind legs. Kangaroos use their hind legs to move themselves forward when they hop. Their ankle bones allow them to absorb the impact from each leap and use it to bounce forward again. Kangaroos can jump almost 9 metres.

SPRINGBOK
HIGHLY SPRUNG

TOP SPEED
60 KPH

1.2 METRES IN LENGTH

AVERAGE WEIGHT
40 KG

LIFESPAN 8 YEARS

FAVOURITE MEAL?

Grass, leaves and roots. A modest diet for these South African sporting greats.

ANNOYING HABIT?

Displaying the hairs on its backside. The springbok has a crest of white fur hidden in a pocket on its back, which stands up when the springbok is in danger. It's an effective way of warning other springboks when there are predators around.

FAVOURITE TRICK?

Sending coded messages. When springboks take flight, their crests create flashes of white above the cloud of dust as they leap and send out a warning to the rest of the herd. And to alert members of the herd looking down as they graze, they also send out special smells that signal danger.

WORST ENEMY?

The cheetah. The only animal to compete with the springbok in the sprint is, unsurprisingly, its chief natural predator. But because this fragile gazelle has more staying power than the big cat, it is often the winner in leaping contests – an amazing achievement!

BIGGEST ADMIRERS?

South African rugby supporters. The springbok has given South Africa's rugby team its name and its symbol. The Springboks' greatest rivals are the Australian Wallabies, who are named after a species of small kangaroo.

MOST IMPRESSIVE FEAT?

Withstanding incredibly high temperatures. Springboks have their own built-in air conditioning. Blood passes through tiny veins in the nose and comes into contact with fresh air in the nostrils as the springbok breathes. This makes the temperature of the blood flowing into the brain drop, and prevents the springbok from overheating. A good way of keeping cool!

SUPERPOWER?

Powerful muscles in its thighs give the springbok its name, which literally means 'sprung deer'. Its back legs are so powerful that a springbok can jump 15 metres in one bound and leap more than 3 metres in the air. Not an easy catch for game hunters! Springboks also jump if they are disturbed, or distressed, a habit known as 'pronking'.

PEREGRINE FALCON
THE FEATHERED MISSILE

TOP SPEED

390 KPH

DIVING SPEED

50 METRES
PER SECOND

AVERAGE WEIGHT 1 KG

WINGSPAN 1 M

LIFESPAN 13 YEARS

When it goes into a dive it drops at a speed of almost 50 m a second. At that speed it's very hard to change course. And if the prey is clever enough, it can dodge the peregrine at the last minute and get away.

BIRTH

Both the mother and father peregrine falcon look after the eggs. When the chicks hatch they are covered in white down. Their nest is not too cosy, usually perched on a high rocky ledge. After a few weeks the chicks begin their strict training. The parents start by giving them chunks of prey to break up, then put bits of food further and further away from the nest to make the chicks fly towards it. A few weeks later, the chicks learn to catch prey in the air, practising on pieces of meat their parents drop for them.

FAVOURITE MEAL?

Other birds. Peregrine falcons like to eat pigeons, crows and gulls. Sometimes the falcon will attack birds bigger than itself. A nice fat goose is a favourite treat.

BEST FRIENDS?

Falconers. The ancient art of falconry is still practised by keen falconers all over the world. They train birds of prey to hunt with them. With their speed and accuracy, peregrines make the ideal hunting partners.

WEAK SPOT?

Aim. Flying at such high speed, the peregrine sometimes misses its prey.

MOST IMPRESSIVE FEAT?

Jumping out of a plane to break a record. That's what a falcon called Frightful did. Until Frightful's owner, no-one had measured how fast peregrine falcons could fly. A mini-computer attached to Frightful clocked her top speed at 390 kph. That's a speed unequalled by birds in the wild, who have to be content with a hunting speed of a mere 190 kph!

SUPERPOWER?

Being able to hunt in mid-air. Falcons are eagle-eyed and can fly at high altitudes out of sight of their prey. But the falcon's dive is the most impressive of all. The peregrine folds its wings and drops from the sky, sometimes free-falling for more than a kilometre. At the last moment it puts on the brakes, collides with its prey and seizes it. And if the victim doesn't die as it's caught, the peregrine finishes it off with its 'killing tooth', a small notch in its beak.

GOLIATH TARANTULA
GIANT BIRD-EATING SPIDER

WEIGHT 130 G

LIFESPAN 20 YEARS

30 CM LONG

LAYS UP TO 1,000 EGGS AT A TIME

TOP SPEED 10 KPH

spiders: earthworms, scorpions and even snakes all feature on its menu. Confusingly, they don't very often eat birds, but were given their name when a Victorian scientist saw one eating a hummingbird.

ANNOYING HABIT?

Bothering entomologists (insect specialists) in the middle of the night. Most spiders move silently but Goliath tarantulas have sharp claws that make a clicking noise when they walk. Harvard University professor Piotr Naskrecki was woken by the sound of a Goliath clicking as he slept in the tropical rainforest. He then discovered that the tarantula had sent out a cloud of hairs with tiny barbs on them that irritated his eyes, and made him cry.

FAVOURITE TRICK?

Ambushing. The Goliath stretches its fine silk across the entrance to its lair and lies in wait. When prey passes nearby, the tarantula is alerted by the vibrations on the web and rushes out of its hole with its venomous claws ready for action.

WORST ENEMY?

The pepsis wasp, also called the tarantula hawk, can paralyse the Goliath with its poison before carrying its victim off to its nest. Instead of devouring the Goliath, the pepsis wasp does something much worse: it lays an egg in its victim's body. Once the larva hatches, it grows inside the living spider and devours it from the inside.

FAVOURITE MEAL?

Its nickname, the birdeater, says a lot about its appetite. Nothing fazes these giant

MOST IMPRESSIVE FEAT?

Terrorising a cinema full of people. In the film *Arachnaphobia*, California is invaded by deadly Goliath spiders. *Arachnophobia* wouldn't scare children living in the Venezualan rainforest though. They like to hunt Goliaths and barbecue them on skewers.

WORST FEATURE?

Being greedy. Females have been known to devour males after mating with them.

SUPERPOWER?

Launching poison arrows. The Goliath has prickly hairs that cause itching and stinging. It sends them out by the hundred when it's threatened as a warning to possible attackers.

PIRANHA
BLOODTHIRSTY BEAST OF LEGEND?

TOP SPEED

40 KPH

30 CM IN LENGTH

1 KG

LIFESPAN **10 YEARS**

ANNOYING HABIT?

Fits of aggression. Piranhas sometimes get trapped in shallow water during the dry season and can become quite ferocious. Their survival instinct kicks in and groups of them will attack anything that crosses their path. They sometimes go for large animals, but most of the time the piranhas themselves end up being eaten by predatory birds.

BIGGEST WEAKNESS?

Being a bundle of nerves. Far from a bloodthirsty monster, the piranha is actually a rather nervous fish. Pet-owners say their piranhas don't like to eat red meat – it upsets their stomach. They prefer a diet of frozen fish.

SILLIEST MISTAKE?

Giving fishermen a terrible fright. Piranhas have been fished out of rivers in mountain villages in France, and have even been discovered in Paris. Finding a carnivorous fish from the Amazon on the other end of your fishing rod is not what you expect when you're doing a spot of weekend fishing. Pet-owners should think twice before dumping the contents of their aquarium.

FAVOURITE MEAL?

Red-bellied piranhas will happily eat dead or dying animals and prey on vulnerable fish, injured animals, and birds that have fallen out of their nests. They have an acute sense of smell and can sniff out a single drop of blood in a large volume of water. With their appetite for dead things, piranhas act as nature's water purifiers: they help to stop the spread of bacteria that develop on rotting dead animals.

SUPERPOWER?

Super-powerful jaws and a mouthful of razor-sharp teeth have given the red-bellied piranha its fearsome reputation as a flesh-eater. Piranhas are capable of stripping a large animal completely down to its skeleton. The legend of man-eating piranhas is as old as the Amazon itself, but there is no real scientific evidence for it. There are plenty of stories though. In December 2013, in Argentina, a group of bathers enjoying a Christmas Day swim got a nasty surprise when a school of piranhas decided to start nibbling on their toes!

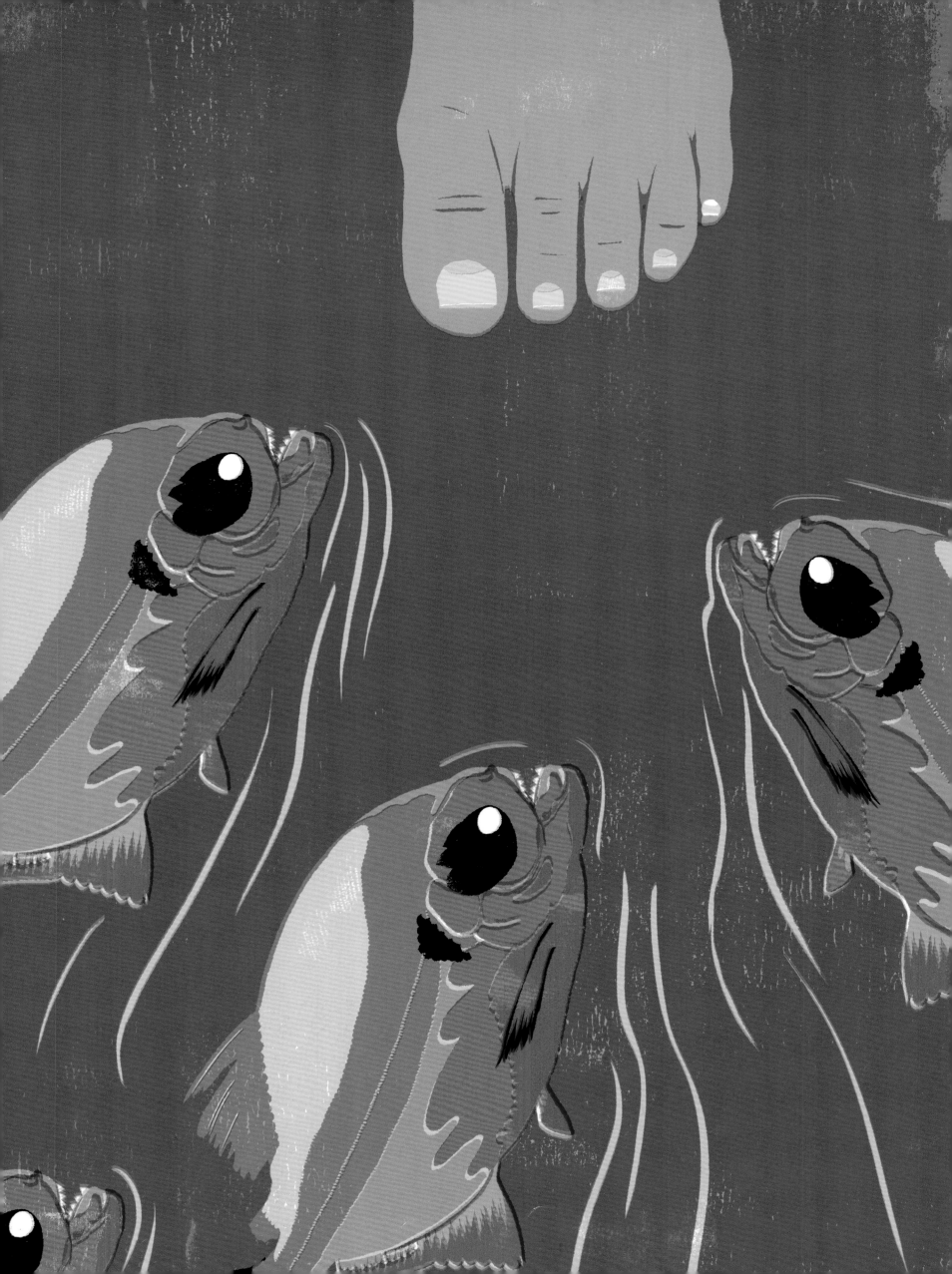

MORAY EEL
ALIEN OF THE DEEP

UP TO **3 METRES** LONG

WEIGHS UP TO **30 KG**

LIFESPAN **15 YEARS**

ANNOYING HABIT?

Biting unsuspecting scuba divers. Moray eels bare their teeth and start biting whenever they feel threatened. Ouch! And when the eel sinks its teeth in and shakes its head around, it can cause a deep wound.

SILLIEST MISTAKE?

Confusing a diver's finger with fish food. Morays don't have very good eyesight and rely mostly on their sense of smell. The moray doesn't think twice about biting the hand that feeds it — something that scuba divers who feed moray eels have learned the hard way!

FAVOURITE TRICK?

Teaming up with another predator to hunt. When a grouper fish is having trouble digging out a small fish from a hole in the rock, it turns to its friend the moray for help. The grouper signals to the moray, and the two work together to catch their victim. They don't even squabble over who gets it.

BEST FRIEND?

The cleaner shrimp, a small crustacean that acts as sort of toothbrush for the moray. This friendly companion helps the moray to get rid of parasites.

FAVOURITE MEAL?

Octopus. Morays can't get enough of their favourite food. If the octopus is really big, the moray pulls off a tentacle by grabbing it with its teeth and spinning round and round at top speed.

WORST FEATURE?

Some moray eels contain high concentrations of *ciguatera* toxin, a naturally occurring poison that can be lethal to humans. These ugly creatures are considered tasty by many, but it is generally agreed that fillet of moray is best avoided.

MOST IMPRESSIVE FEAT?

Dancing with divers! Divers who return often to the same waters have been known to befriend these odd-looking creatures. When the moray sees the diver coming, it slithers up and slides in and out of the diver's arms to be stroked as it dances.

SUPERPOWER?

Alien jaws. The moray is equipped with a mouthful of sharp teeth coated in toxic saliva. One species of American moray has a second set of jaws in its throat. When the moray has prey in its mouth, the second set of jaws comes up out of the throat like a pair of deadly, sharp-toothed pliers and pulls the prey straight down towards the stomach.

VAMPIRE BAT
WORST NIGHTMARE COME TRUE

TOP SPEED
15 KPH

WINGSPAN 30 CM

WEIGHS UP TO
50 G

LIFESPAN 15 YEARS

MOST IMPRESSIVE FEAT?

Helping humans! Vampire saliva contains *draculin*, a substance that stops blood from clotting. Scientists are studying *draculin* as it may be useful for preventing blood clots, a major cause of heart attacks and strokes.

BIGGEST MISTAKE?

Attacking humans. In 2010, Wampi Indians living in the Peruvian forest were stormed by a swarm of vampire bats. Many of the victims could not get help quickly enough and died of a disease called rabies. You can see why people might be tempted to believe those tales of man-eating bats in the Amazon rainforest.

FAVOURITE TRICK?

Moving undetected along the ground. Vampire bats can move very fast on solid ground. They can walk, run, go backwards, jump and climb. They can even take off by leaping straight up into the air.

WORST ENEMY?

Farmers. Vampire bats often attack livestock in South America. Animals bitten by vampire bats become weak from loss of blood and die of diseases carried by the bats. It's a real problem for cattle ranchers and farmers.

FAVOURITE MEAL?

Fresh blood. Vampire bats drink blood from mammals at night. They pierce the victim's skin with their razor-sharp teeth and drink its blood using their tongue as a straw. The bat sometimes gorges itself on blood so much that it has a hard time flying off again. It has to wait until it has digested its meal before travelling back to its favourite cave.

WEAK SPOT?

Food. Vampire bats can't go for very long without feeding. They rely on the blood they drink for *haemoglobin* and can die after just two days without a fresh supply. But being very community-minded little beasts, the bats have a solution. If a vampire doesn't manage to find any prey, another bat will help it out by spitting up a few mouthfuls of blood directly into its mouth.

SUPERPOWER?

Vampire bats are covered in millions of sensors. Heat sensors near the nose are used for locating warm-blooded animals, and super-sensitive whisker-like hairs can detect the slightest movement in their prey. At night, bats navigate by *echolocation*, a system of radar that uses sound waves.

FOX
MASTER OF DECEPTION

1 METRE FROM NOSE TO TAIL

TOP SPEED
60 KPH

7 KG

LIFESPAN 5 YEARS

ANNOYING HABIT?

Stealing everything it can lay its paws on: golf balls, picnics, rubbish, left-overs ... Foxes will even come in to people's houses looking for loot. In London, there have been reports of foxes attacking small children as they sleep, but fortunately this is extremely rare.

WORST FEATURE?

Eating hens. A fox will do anything to break into a hen-house, from digging a hole under the fence to cutting through chicken wire with its teeth, or just jumping over the fence. Farmers have to make sure they lock all the doors at night when their chickens come home to roost.

FAVOURITE TRICK?

Playing dead. Cunning Mr Fox has been known to use this trick to trap crows and even to fool hunters. The fox falls down and pretends to be wounded after a shot is fired. As soon as the hunter has put down his gun, the fox jumps up and runs away.

WORST ENEMY?

The fox terrier. For hundreds of years, these little dogs have been used to help men drive foxes from their lair. The terrier digs down underground and corners the fox, which can then be forced out with the aid of shovels and pickaxes. And there's usually a gunshot after that.

FAVOURITE MEAL?

Foxes love voles and field mice but they'll eat just about anything. Foxes that live in towns particularly like raiding rubbish bins.

MOST IMPRESSIVE FEAT?

Being a living legend. Reynard The Fox is the main character in a series of Medieval animal tales, most of which recount the tricks Reynard uses to outwit people and other animals. He is particularly fond of duping his cousin, Ysengrin the wolf.

SUPERPOWER?

Detecting prey in just about all conditions. The fox has super-powerful senses and can locate rodents that think they're safe in their underground tunnels. The fox can even sniff out a mouse through one metre of snow. Once the fox has the mouse in the open, it leaps high in the air and lands on its prey so it can't move.

BROWN RAT

LORD OF NEW YORK AND PARIS

TOP SPEED

13 KPH

40 CM FROM NOSE TO TAIL

400 G

LIFESPAN 2 YEARS

BIRTH

Rats win hands down at multiplication. Each litter can contain as many as ten baby rats. With six litters a year, one female rat can produce 2,500 offspring in her lifetime. The babies are weaned at about four weeks and then trained by an adult of the same sex who teaches them the rules of rat life.

ANNOYING HABIT?

Gnawing on everything they can get their teeth into, including cardboard, soap, electric cables and phone lines. Rats have been known to cause major power blackouts. In Japan the damaged Fukushima nuclear power plant had to shut down its cooling plant when a rat chewed through a switchboard.

WORST ENEMY?

Man. People are always trying to trap rats by any means possible. But rats actually do a great deal for humans. They do their bit to keep sewers unblocked and can even help with landmine detection. Rats have an amazing sense of smell and have been used to sniff out landmines in Africa. Areas that were once warzones are now much safer, thanks to these rodents.

MOST IMPRESSIVE FEAT?

Spanning the globe. Rats came originally from Asia. They stowed away on Viking longships almost a thousand years ago and spread throughout the whole planet. Nowadays they are everywhere. There are stylish rat residences in the sewers of Paris, where rat colonies consume thousands of tonnes of waste every year. And in New York, even the coolest of cats are no match for the rats who make the most of their free pass on the subway system.

WORST FEATURE?

Spreading diseases. Rats carry all sorts of viruses and parasites that cause diseases. The flea of the black rat was responsible for the Black Death, an outbreak of a disease called bubonic plague that killed millions of people in Europe in the Middle Ages. The plague still claims victims in parts of the world today.

SUPERPOWER?

Collective intelligence. Rats communicate with each other using calls too high for the human ear to hear. They collaborate on group strategies and can alert each other to the presence of danger. When a colony of rats encounter unfamiliar food, they send out tasters that risk their lives by testing the food for poison!

OCTOPUS
TENTACULAR INTELLIGENCE

70 CM
IN DIAMETER

LIFESPAN **2 YEARS**

6 KG

TOP SPEED **7 KPH**

pursued. The Mimic octopus can even put off predators by making itself look like other marine creatures, such as the venomous sea snake.

BIRTH

Octopus parents both die soon after the young are born and the orphans have to learn to survive on their own. They watch the behaviour of their fellow octopuses and learn very quickly. An octopus only needs to find its way through a maze once and it will remember the route for life.

ANNOYING HABIT?

Using its ink to muddy the waters. The octopus has an ink sac, a bag near its middle where it stores black ink. It's a highly effective weapon that allows it to escape predators in a cloud of black fog. The cloud it sends out is almost the same size and shape as the octopus itself.

SILLIEST MISTAKE?

Stealing a camera. A diver filming in deep water in New Zealand suddenly found himself empty-handed. An octopus had borrowed his equipment and used it to make its own video.

FAVOURITE TRICK?

Camouflage. The octopus has special cells under its skin that allow it to mimic the colour and texture of its environment. It can camouflage itself when it hunts or when it is being

FAVOURITE MEAL?

Crabs and crustaceans. The octopus has a big appetite and can practically double its weight in three months.

MOST IMPRESSIVE FEAT?

Predicting the results of the World Cup. In 2010, before each match, Paul the Octopus had to choose between two boxes, each containing the flag of one of the teams in the match. Paul correctly predicted all seven of Germany's World Cup victories.

SUPERPOWER?

A very high IQ. Each of the octopus's eight tentacles contains a sort of mini brain. When scientists tested octopus tentacles kept in very cold water, they found that the tentacles reacted to being prodded even after they had been separated from the body.

DOLPHIN
BRAINS OF THE SEA

TOP SPEED

50 KPH

UP TO

4 METRES

IN LENGTH

WEIGHS UP TO

400 KG

LIFESPAN 30 YEARS

BIRTH

After a 12-month pregnancy, the mother dolphin gives birth to a single baby. Without air the calf would drown, so the mother helps it swim to the surface to take its first gulp. The calf suckles its mother for more than a year before starting to fend for itself. There's nothing odd about this: dolphins are mammals, not fish.

ANNOYING HABIT?

Making funny noises all the time. A dolphin is a real live musical box. Tourists love to listen to dolphins' non-stop clicks and whistles.

WORST ENEMY?

Fishing hooks and nets. Dolphins can get caught up in fishing lines, but fortunately they often get away. One dolphin asked a passing diver for help by signalling with its fin that it needed to be set free from a fishing line.

MOST IMPRESSIVE FEAT?

Protecting humans. Dolphins have come to the aid of people under threat from sharks on several occasions. Even the biggest sharks don't like being hit with a dolphin's snout. Dolphins have a long bony nose like a beak that can cause lethal injuries to sharks.

FAVOURITE TRICK?

Circling their prey. Dolphins like to hunt in packs. When they spot a school of mackerel they circle it and force the fish to the surface. Every dolphin has its part to play. Beaters strike the water with their tails to round up the prey, while guards make sure no fish escape. Then it's just a matter of taking turns to charge at the dazed fish with mouths wide open.

FAVOURITE MEAL?

Fish and squid. Dolphins use their teeth to seize slippery prey but they can't chew – they don't have enough muscles in their jaws. However, they do have two or three stomachs to help them digest up to 8 kg of food a day. They're seafood fanatics!

BEST FEATURE?

Being very intelligent. Unfortunately their intelligence is the very reason why they are often to be found in captivity.

SUPERPOWER?

Sonar equipment. The dolphin has a lump on its forehead called a melon that means it can make sounds. The sound creates a wave in the water that bounces against obstacles and creates an echo, which the dolphin uses to locate its prey. It also allows the dolphin to be aware of potential predators.

KING COBRA
A ROYAL MENACE

LIFESPAN
20 YEARS

TOP SPEED
20 KPH

4 METRES
LONG

50 CM
AT BIRTH

6 KG

WORST ENEMY?

The mongoose. The mongoose loves to eat cobra eggs and is the only mammal to stand up to the serpent king of the Indian jungle. Leeches also like to feast on cobra. These little parasites aren't really afraid of anything, and even the all-powerful king cobra can do nothing to fend them off.

BIRTH

The cobra likes to hatch its eggs in comfort. It builds a nest of bamboo leaves, a rare habit in the snake world. The baby snakes, already half a metre in length, come out of their shells by the dozen, already stripey. Their mother quickly disappears to avoid the temptation of devouring her offspring – the king cobra eats mostly snakes.

FAVOURITE TRICK?

Lying in wait in a tree. The cobra's long, forked tongue detects smells in the air and works out what they are using a specially adapted organ in its mouth known as Jacobson's organ. The brain receives the message that prey is approaching and then prepares for an immediate attack.

BEST FRIENDS?

Villagers in Ban Khok Sa-nga. This village in Thailand is nicknamed 'Cobra Village', because every household keeps a cobra. The cobras are fed and pampered by their owners who think nothing of squaring up to them as they rear up. The most fearless of villagers even kiss their pets on the mouth. Not surprisingly people have lost their lives in this 'kiss of death' game. The villagers make money by running live shows to entertain tourists.

QUIRK OF CHARACTER?

The cobra is very territorial. It would rather defend its nest than slither off, like a viper does when threatened. And the cobra can stand up to most enemies. A full-sized king cobra can be more than 4 metres long – big enough to look an adult man in the eye when it rears up.

SUPERPOWER?
Plus-size venom glands. A cobra's glands contain about two teaspoonfuls of venom, enough to kill several dozen adult men. And the symptoms are gruesome: paralysis, blurred vision, heart attack and an inability to breathe.

BOX JELLYFISH
KILLS IN FIVE MINUTES

TOP SPEED **7 KPH**

3 METRES LONG, INCLUDING TENTACLES

 COMPOSITION **90 %** WATER

2 KG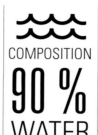

LIFESPAN 9 MONTHS

FAVOURITE MEAL?

Tiny shrimp that live in sandbanks close to Australian beaches. Unfortunately people like to swim here too. In some resorts, there are anti-jellyfish nets to stop these uninvited guests from giving children paddling in the sea a nasty surprise.

ANNOYING HABIT?

Swimming around with its tentacles floating along behind: a killer habit for people enjoying a swim. Jellyfish stings kill about 50 people every year, far more than sharks do. Quite a feat for creatures made up of 90 per cent water.

these rubbery creatures could well extend their reach to other parts of the world.

WORST ENEMY?

Turtles. Turtles love jellyfish, even the deadly ones. They can digest the ultra-toxic venom of the box jelly without so much as a hiccough. The box jellyfish's only defence other than its tentacles is its eyesight. One of the few jellyfish to have real eyes, the box jelly has an impressive total of 24 eyes.

FAVOURITE TRICK?

Using jet propulsion to chase after prey and catch it in its tentacles, a trick not many jellyfish can perform. Most would rather just drift along with the currents. Box jellyfish can move through the water at speeds of up to four knots – as fast as an average human swims.

WORST FEATURE?

A terrible reputation. The box jellyfish is reputed to be the deadliest creature on the planet. The good news is that there is an effective anti-venom serum. The bad news is that it takes the serum 15 minutes to act while jellyfish venom can cause a heart attack within five minutes.

BEST FRIEND?

Ocean currents. The world's deadliest jellyfish live off the coast of northern Australia but with new warm currents created by global warming,

SUPERPOWER?

Armfuls of miniature syringes. Each tentacle is loaded with thousands of tiny barbs, ready to be launched at the slightest touch. The barbs release drops of venom, rather like a stinging nettle does. In some places, the box jellyfish is known as the 'hand of death' because of the horrible injuries it inflicts on its victims. The sting is painful and often fatal. However, applying vinegar stops the venom from doing its deadly work.

STONEFISH
A PRICKLY CHARACTER

3 KPH

30 CM IN LENGTH

2.5 KG

LIFESPAN 7 YEARS

MOST SPECTACULAR FEAT?

Being able to live for as long as 24 hours out of the water, thanks to a system of special gills, which also prevents it from swallowing sand when it's lying in wait for prey.

WEAK SPOT?

Its bulging eyes. A stonefish's eyes protrude from the top of its head and aren't camouflaged. A must for divers to know, and look out for. It's not impossible for a diver with a practised eye to spot a stonefish.

SILLIEST MISTAKE?

Getting caught in nets, like an ordinary stone. Not a good catch for the fisherman who grabs it to throw it back into the water. But a fisherman who knows what he's doing can feast on the stonefish's tasty flesh. Delicious when seasoned with garlic and ginger, after the spines have been removed, of course!

FAVOURITE TRICK?

Camouflage and surprise. The stonefish is perfectly dressed to blend into the scenery. Marine debris clings to its sticky skin as it sits on rocks or the sandy seabed, making it practically invisible. This expert camouflage artist doesn't swim very much. It is happy to sit and wait until prey passes by and then grab it with lightning speed. It all happens in one hundredth of a second, one of the fastest moves in the animal kingdom.

FAVOURITE MEAL?

The stonefish is very greedy and eats shrimp and little fish. It can swallow prey almost as big as itself.

WORST FEATURE?

Its looks! The stonefish is horribly ugly. Its scientific name means 'covered in warts' which just about says it all! Perhaps that's why it tries to stay hidden.

SUPERPOWER?

Thirteen dorsal spines. Each of the stonefish's spines has a sac of venom that is as deadly as a cobra's venom. The spines stick up at the slightest sign of danger. If you want to go exploring at low tide in tropical lagoons favoured by stonefish, make sure you're wearing a pair of thick-soled shoes. Stonefish can pierce right through ordinary flip-flops.

GOLDEN POISON DART FROG
BEAUTIFUL BUT DEADLY

5 CM IN LENGTH

LIFESPAN 5 YEARS

TOP SPEED 2 KPH

BIRTH

Poison dart frogs are brought up by their dad. When the tadpoles hatch, their father carries them on his back and takes them to a pool where they gradually transform into young adults. Fifty-five days later, the young frogs are ready to leave the water.

WORST ENEMY?

The tree snake, the only inhabitant of the Colombian rainforests able to eat the frog's deadly toxin and survive. The snake dines mostly on baby frogs.

BIGGEST WEAKNESS?

Being sought after all over the world. Illegal traffic is common between industrialised countries and the rainforests of the Amazon. Poison dart frogs make popular exotic pets and are also used in medical research. Their deadly poison contains a pain-killing substance that is believed to be more effective than any existing painkiller.

WEAK SPOT?

Losing their powers in captivity. In the wild, the poison dart frog feeds on insects and makes its venom from toxins in its diet. After a few weeks in captivity on a diet of harmless crickets, the frog loses its toxicity. Fortunately there are no predators around; the only thing it has to fear is boredom.

FAVOURITE TRICK?

Displaying its colours. The frog's bright skin is a warning to predators: 'Touch me and you'll be poisoned.' This form of dissuasion, the opposite of camouflage, is used by many animals and has a long name: 'aposematism'. Hornets, snakes, fish and insects, for example, also use it to let people know that it's definitely a bad idea to touch them.

SUPERPOWER?

The poison dart frog's Latin name contains the word "terribilis", which needs no translating. This little frog has enough venom to kill up to 20 humans. More powerful even than the toxic substance curare, frog poison is used by some people in the rainforests of Colombia to poison their arrows, which is where the frog gets its name. The tip of the arrow is rubbed along the frog's back. Alternatively the frogs are grilled on skewers to make them sweat out their poison. The ultimate lethal weapon!